MEERKATS

by *Josh Gregory*

Children's Press®

An Imprint of Scholastic Inc.

Content Consultant
Dr. Stephen S. Ditchkoff
Professor of Wildlife Ecology and Management
Auburn University
Auburn, Alabama

Library of Congress Cataloging-in-Publication Data
Gregory, Josh, author.
 Meerkats / by Josh Gregory.
  pages cm. — (Nature's children)
 Summary: "This book details the life and habits of meerkats"—
Provided by publisher.
 Includes bibliographical references and index.
 ISBN 978-0-531-22721-3 (library binding : alk. paper) —
 ISBN 978-0-531-22519-6 (pbk. : alk. paper)
1. Meerkat—Juvenile literature. I. Title. II. Series: Nature's children
(New York, N.Y.)
 QL737.C235G74 2016
 599.74'2—dc23   2015020024

Printed in China 62
SCHOLASTIC, CHILDREN'S PRESS, and associated logos are
trademarks and/or registered trademarks of Scholastic Inc.

1 2 3 4 5 6 7 8 9 10 R 25 24 23 22 21 20 19 18 17 16

Meerkats

Class	Mammalia
Order	Carnivora
Family	Herpestidae
Genus	*Suricata*
Species	*Suricata suricatta*
World distribution	Southwestern Africa
Habitat	Dry plains and grasslands
Distinctive physical characteristics	Long, thin bodies; around 9.75 to 11.75 inches (25 to 30 centimeters) tall, with a tail measuring 7.5 to 9.5 inches (19 to 24 cm); weighs less than 2.2 pounds (1 kilogram); females are usually slightly larger than males; covered in fur that ranges in color from gray to tan, with darker markings along the back and at the tip of the tail; dark coloring around eyes and ears
Habits	Lives with other meerkats in family groups of 3 to 50 members; digs elaborate burrow systems; has a complex social system; diurnal; spends five to eight hours per day foraging for food; relies on other group members to look out for threats while foraging; helps care for offspring of fellow group members; is territorial against rival meerkat groups
Diet	Primarily eats insects and arachnids, including termites, spiders, scorpions, and beetles; also eats small lizards, snakes, birds, and rodents; sometimes eats eggs and fruit

Contents

CHAPTER 1

On the Lookout

The sun beats down on the dusty grasslands of southern Africa's Kalahari Desert. Amid the shrubs and patches of rocky dirt, there is a flurry of activity. A group of small, furry animals is sniffing around and pawing at the ground. It is a family of meerkats! They are on the lookout for a tasty meal. Little do the meerkats know that another predator plans to make them its own dinner. Off in the distance, a wild dog called a jackal is sneaking toward them.

Standing atop a tall rock, one of the meerkats has not been searching for food. Instead, she has risen up tall on her back legs and is looking out over the surrounding area. She spots the approaching jackal and lets out a warning noise, then quickly takes off running. The other meerkats drop what they are doing and sprint toward a hole in the ground. Danger has been avoided!

Meerkats keep a watchful eye over their surroundings to help protect one another.

Tall, Thin, and Furry

Meerkats are small mammals with long, thin bodies. On average, they are about 9.75 to 11.75 inches (25 to 30 centimeters) tall when standing on their rear legs. They also have skinny tails that measure an additional 7.5 to 9.5 inches (19 to 24 cm). Meerkats are very lightweight, generally weighing less than 2.2 pounds (1 kilogram). Females tend to be slightly larger than males, but the difference between them is not immediately noticeable.

A meerkat's body is completely covered in a layer of fuzzy fur. Most of the fur is various shades of tan and gray. The animal's back and tail usually have darker coloring than its underside. It also has dark fur around its eyes and on its ears.

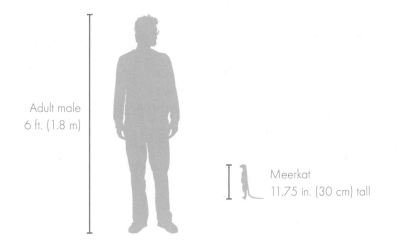

Adult male
6 ft. (1.8 m)

Meerkat
11.75 in. (30 cm) tall

Meerkats' tall, slender bodies make them highly agile.

Desert Dwellers

Meerkats live throughout much of southwestern Africa in an area known as the Kalahari Desert. Though the Kalahari Desert is fairly dry, it is not a true desert. It does receive some rain, and there are many plants and animals living throughout the region. A huge variety of grasses and shrubs poke up from the sandy, reddish dirt. Taller trees dot the landscape. Flat plains stretch on for long distances, occasionally interrupted by hills of sand.

Temperatures in the Kalahari Desert can reach up to 115 degrees Fahrenheit (46 degrees Celsius) on a summer day. But it can become quite cold in the winter. Meerkats deal with these temperature extremes—and stay safe from predators—by building burrows underground. The temperature inside the burrows is cool on hot days and warm during cold nights.

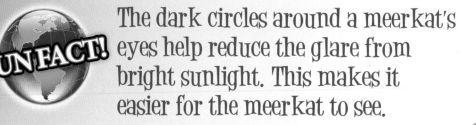

FUN FACT! The dark circles around a meerkat's eyes help reduce the glare from bright sunlight. This makes it easier for the meerkat to see.

Meerkats blend in well with their sandy homes.

Digging Deep

With long, thin bodies that easily fit through narrow tunnels, meerkats are perfectly suited to life in their underground homes. Sometimes they live in burrows that were dug by other animals, such as South African ground squirrels. Other times, they build their own homes. To do this, they use the four long claws on each of their front paws to scoop out dirt. Then they kick the dirt behind them. As they dig, meerkats can close their ears to keep dirt from getting inside. They also have special membranes that protect their eyes as they work.

Meerkat burrows are often complex structures. They have many different rooms connected by a series of tunnels. There are usually several levels to a burrow. The deepest parts may reach up to 6.5 feet (2 meters) below the surface. Different rooms have different purposes. Some are used as toilet areas, while others are for sleeping. Each burrow has many entrances. This allows meerkats to reach a close entrance and go underground quickly when danger approaches. It also prevents them from getting trapped inside.

Burrows help meerkats stay safe and give them a place to get out of the desert heat.

CHAPTER 2

Relying on One Another

Meerkats live together in family groups called mobs or gangs. Each mob might be made up of anywhere from 3 to 50 meerkats. The members of these groups rely on one another in almost every aspect of their lives. They help one another care for babies, avoid danger, and find food.

Meerkats eat many different types of food. Technically, they are omnivores. This means they eat both animals and plants. Plants make up a very small part of a meerkat's diet, however. Most meals consist of insects and arachnids. Some favorite foods include scorpions, termites, beetles, and spiders. Though many of these animals are venomous, meerkats do not need to fear being poisoned. They are immune to many of these defenses. Meerkats also eat small lizards, snakes, toads, and even birds or rodents. When the weather is especially dry, they might dig up plant roots that have a lot of moisture in them.

A lizard makes a tasty meal for a hungry meerkat.

Foraging Techniques

Meerkats spend a lot of time looking for things to eat. On an average day, a meerkat might spend anywhere from five to eight hours foraging. Each mob has several different foraging areas. The mobs visit a new area each day until they have used them all. The process then starts over from the beginning. This prevents mobs from wiping out all the food sources in a certain area.

Meerkat mobs spread out as they search for food. Individuals keep several feet of space between one another most of the time. As they hunt, they continually communicate with one another using soft sounds. Most of their prey is located underground, beneath rocks, or in other out-of-the-way places. To track these animals down, meerkats rely on their sense of smell. When they find something, they use their powerful claws to dig it up and kill it.

Each meerkat finds most of its own food. Group members, however, sometimes share larger prey. They might even band together to kill something that is too big for a single meerkat to handle. Other times, a meerkat might sneak up and steal food from one of its fellow group members.

Many of a meerkat's favorite foods are found underground.

Staying Safe

The Kalahari Desert is home to many predators that see meerkats as tasty snacks. Jackals are one common enemy. Others include hawks and eagles, which swoop down out of the sky to snatch meerkats from the ground. While meerkats are safe from such attacks when in their burrows, coming out to forage leaves them vulnerable. That is why at least one meerkat always stands guard. The meerkats take turns in this position, relieving each other once they have eaten their fill. While guarding, a meerkat climbs to the highest point it can reach and stands tall on its rear legs. If the meerkat sees danger, it lets out a warning call. There are different warning sounds for different kinds of predators. This way, the meerkats know whether they need to avoid an attack from the ground or the sky.

Meerkats cannot escape all predators by fleeing underground. Snakes can fit inside meerkat burrows and attack them. As a result, meerkats must avoid letting snakes come near tunnel entrances. When a snake is spotted, nearby mob members gang up and attack it. With any luck, either the snake will retreat or the mob will kill it.

Snakes can be both predators and prey for meerkats.

Turf Wars

A mob's burrows and foraging places are all located within an area called a home range. This area takes up about 4 square miles (10 square kilometers) on average. Meerkats mark their group's territory by rubbing their scent glands on rocks and other objects. This leaves a distinctive smell behind.

Parts of one mob's home range often overlap with others. As a result, different mobs sometimes encounter each other as they go about their daily business. Mobs often come into conflict when they meet. Members of rival groups might try to steal each other's mates or food. At first, the mobs try to threaten each other away. They get down on all fours and stick their tails straight up toward the sky. Then they jump forward at each other. This often scares away one of the mobs. The meeting will turn violent, however, if neither group backs off. The meerkats will fight each other, and some of them might even die in the battle.

Meerkats can be extremely vicious when defending their territory from rival mobs.

CHAPTER 3

Mob Life

As the sun rises, a meerkat mob gets ready to start the day. The members crawl out of their burrow and into the warmth of the morning sun. They might then spend some time socializing with one another. They play, relax, and groom each other. This helps strengthen the bonds between family members. The meerkats can recognize individuals in their group by their smells. Each meerkat has a distinct personality and role within the group.

Eventually, the group will start foraging. This activity takes up most of the day. However, a meerkat might take a break to cool off in a shady spot or take a short nap underground.

As the sun sets, the meerkats are tired out from the day's activities. One by one, they return to the burrow. There, they curl up together in sleeping chambers to sleep and prepare for another day.

Meerkats show affection for their fellow mob members in many ways.

Meerkat Mating

The social structure of a meerkat mob plays a huge role in determining which members mate and have babies. Each group has a **dominant** male and a dominant female. The dominant male fights the other males in the group. He tries to keep them from mating with the females. Similarly, the dominant female tries to prevent the other females from becoming pregnant. If another female does become pregnant, the dominant female might chase her out of the group or even kill her. As a result, the dominant female is the mother of around 80 percent of the babies born in the group. The dominant male is usually the father.

Sometimes a nondominant female is able to successfully mate and have babies without conflict. However, that doesn't mean the risk is over. The dominant female might try to kill the babies, especially if she is about to have her own **litter**. Additionally, nondominant females might try to kill one another's newborn pups or even the pups of the dominant female.

A pregnant meerkat is easy to spot because of its large, round belly.

A Family Affair

Meerkat mothers give birth to a litter of three or four babies. These pups are born about 11 weeks after their parents mate. A meerkat might reproduce up to three times each year. This is why meerkats try not to let each other have too many pups. If all the females had several pups each year, a group would grow too large too quickly. There would not be enough resources to go around.

Although meerkats can be vicious and competitive in determining which members get to reproduce, they are very caring when it comes to raising young. The entire group works together. Relatives babysit growing pups when the parents are foraging. The group's adults all help teach the pups which kinds of food to eat and how to attack prey. They also protect the young meerkats from threats and show them how to escape predators.

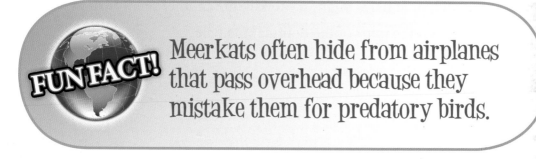

FUN FACT! Meerkats often hide from airplanes that pass overhead because they mistake them for predatory birds.

Young meerkats are rarely far from an adult family member.

Learning and Growing

Meerkat pups are born very small. Their eyes are closed, and they don't have much fur. At first, they live on a diet of milk from their mother. They stay in their burrow to avoid danger, as they would be easy targets for predators outside. When they are roughly three weeks old, family members start bringing them solid food to eat along with the milk. About a week later, the pups start leaving the burrow to explore the world outside. There, they spend time playing and observing the group's adults. At first, they beg for food by squeaking at their relatives. They soon stop drinking milk. As they grow and learn, they begin foraging on their own.

Meerkats reach adulthood when they are about a year old. At this time, males might leave and try to join a group where they have a better chance of mating. Females stay with their mobs. They help raise future babies and perhaps even have young of their own. In the wild, an average meerkat might live for about 10 years.

Once they are a couple of weeks old, baby meerkats look like tiny versions of adults.

CHAPTER 4

Meerkats and Mongooses

Though their names might sound alike, meerkats are not related to cats. Instead, they belong to a family of animals called mongooses. There are 33 mongoose species living today. Scientists organize them into 18 genera. The meerkat is one of these species. It is the only animal that belongs to the genus *Suricata*.

All mongooses share a basic physical resemblance to meerkats. They have long, thin bodies. They also have pointy faces, short legs, and narrow tails. Different species vary in size. The tiny dwarf mongoose measures only about 12.6 to 17.3 inches (32 to 44 cm) from its nose to the tip of its tail. At the other extreme, the white-tailed mongoose is about three times that length.

Like meerkats, other mongooses are strong predators. Some species regularly battle one-on-one with some of the world's most dangerous venomous snakes.

Mongooses show no fear when faced with a battle against a deadly snake.

Ancient Relatives

Today, most mongoose species are found throughout the continent of Africa. Several species live only on the island nation of Madagascar, which lies off Africa's southeastern coast. A few species in the genus *Herpestes* can be found in parts of southern Europe and southern Asia.

All mongooses share **ancestors** that probably lived in Europe tens of millions of years ago. Many other modern animals share these same ancestors, including dogs, bears, and weasels. Early mongooses probably made their way from Europe to Africa around 20 million years ago. From there, some ancient mongooses probably spread to the other locations where these animals are found today.

Scientists have learned about the history of the mongoose by studying **fossils**. One factor they study is how old fossils are in different parts of the world. This tells scientists where mongoose ancestors lived at different times. The fossils also reveal what these ancient animals probably looked like and even how they may have lived.

The ring-tailed mongoose is one of the many mongoose species living today.

Red or Yellow?

Meerkats have a few features that set them apart from the other mongoose species living today. Most mongoose species have five toes on each foot. Meerkats have just four. Other mongooses also tend to have larger ears and thicker fur than meerkats have.

Meerkats share the most similarities with the yellow mongoose. In fact, these two species are so alike that the yellow mongoose is also known as the red meerkat. Both names come from its dark yellow fur, which often has a reddish tint.

Like the meerkat, the yellow mongoose has four toes on each of its back feet. But like other mongooses, it has five toes on each of its front feet. It also has the larger ears and thicker fur that other mongooses possess. Nevertheless, meerkats and yellow mongooses are similar enough that the two species have sometimes shared burrows.

Unless you know which differences to look for, it is easy to mistake a yellow mongoose for a meerkat.

CHAPTER 5

When Humans Meet Meerkats

Meerkats have a playful, curious nature. They also have a cute appearance and a fascinating way of living. As a result, these remarkable animals are quick to catch humans' attention. They are a very popular attraction at zoos, where huge crowds gather to watch meerkat families in action. Meerkats have also been the subjects of popular nature shows on television. They are even portrayed as funny characters in cartoons and advertisements.

Because of this popularity, some people develop an interest in keeping meerkats as pets. Many people also like to use them to help control pests in their gardens or yards. Skilled trainers can make these wild animals somewhat tame, and meerkat owners enjoy their company at first. However, meerkats are challenging pets. Many problems can arise when people take them out of their natural habitats.

Meerkats' playfulness and intelligence make them very fun to watch.

Born to Be Wild

Meerkats can be very unpleasant to live with. They appear cute and cuddly. However, they can suddenly lash out and become violent if they are frightened or confused. Meerkats have long, pointy teeth that are meant to tear through prey. A bite from these teeth can be very painful.

A meerkat's instinct to dig and scratch around for prey can also cause problems. Meerkats are likely to damage homes when they are brought indoors. They tear up carpets and chew on anything they can find. This can even result in a meerkat hurting itself by eating something dangerous or biting an electrical cable.

Perhaps worst of all, meerkats are not used to living by themselves. They need constant interaction with their family members to stay happy and healthy. Meerkats often become depressed when they are forced to live in cages. They might start to hurt themselves by pulling out their own fur or chewing on their legs.

Meerkats' digging behavior is one of many reasons these animals do not make good pets.

Making Room for Meerkats

Many people who try to keep meerkats as pets eventually decide to give them up. However, it is not easy to find a home for an unwanted meerkat. Because they are not used to living in the wild, pet meerkats cannot simply be returned to their natural homes. Often, the best place for these pets is in refuges where they can receive proper care.

It is better to observe meerkats from afar, allowing them to continue thriving in their natural homes. Wild meerkat populations are very healthy. They face little risk of becoming endangered anytime soon. Many of these animals even live in parks or other areas. In these places, rules protect the animals from any potential harm by humans. By treating this fascinating species with care and respect, we can help make sure that meerkats continue to live safely and thrive.

Researchers continue to study meerkats and learn more about how these amazing animals live.

Words to Know

ancestors (AN-ses-turz) — ancient animal species that are related to modern species

arachnids (uh-RAK-nidz) — animals such as spiders and scorpions, with eight legs and a body divided into two segments

burrows (BUR-ohz) — tunnels or holes in the ground made or used as a home by an animal

dominant (DAH-muh-nint) — most influential or powerful

endangered (en-DAYN-jurd) — at risk of becoming extinct, usually because of human activity

foraging (FOR-ij-ing) — going in search of food

fossils (FOSS-uhlz) — the hardened remains of prehistoric plants and animals

genera (JEN-ur-uh) — groups of related plants or animals that are larger than a species but smaller than a family

glands (GLANDZ) — organs in the body that produce or release natural chemicals

groom (GROOM) — to brush and clean

habitats (HAB-uh-tats) — places where an animal or a plant is usually found

home range (HOME RAYNJ) — an area of land in which an animal spends most of its time

immune (i-MYOON) — if you are immune to a disease, you don't get sick from it

litter (LIT-ur) — a number of baby animals that are born at the same time to the same mother

mammals (MAM-uhlz) — warm-blooded animals that have hair or fur and usually give birth to live young

mates (MAYTS) — animals that join together to produce babies

membranes (MEM-braynz) — very thin layers of tissue that line or cover certain organs or cells

omnivores (AHM-nuh-vorz) — animals that eat both plants and meat

predator (PRED-uh-tur) — an animal that lives by hunting other animals for food

prey (PRAY) — an animal that's hunted by another animal for food

refuges (REF-yooj-iz) — places that provide protection or shelter

species (SPEE-sheez) — one of the groups into which animals and plants of the same genus are divided; members of the same species can mate and have offspring

venomous (VEN-uhm-us) — able to produce poison that is usually passed into a victim's body through a bite or sting

Habitat Map

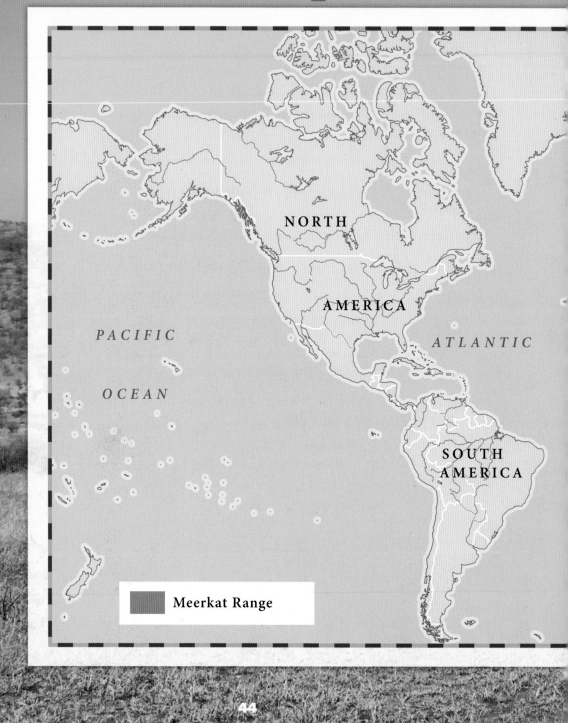

NORTH

AMERICA

PACIFIC

OCEAN

ATLANTIC

SOUTH
AMERICA

Meerkat Range

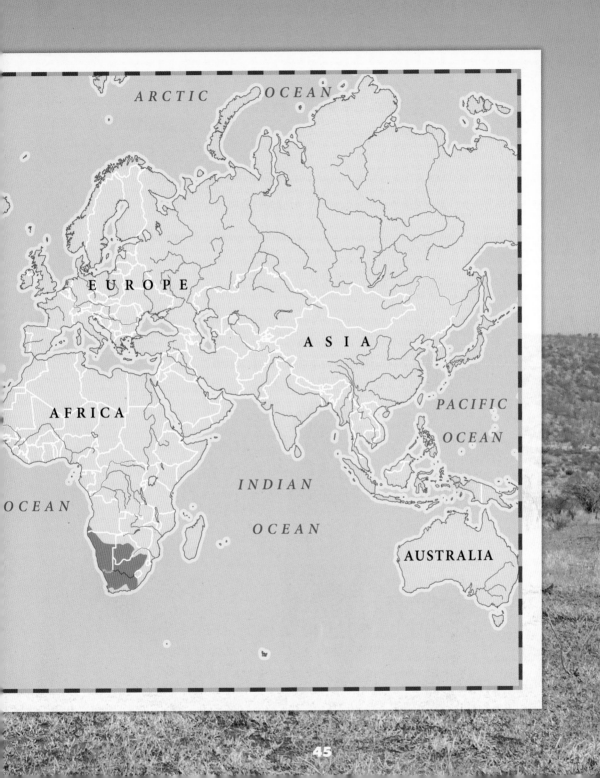

ARCTIC OCEAN

EUROPE

ASIA

AFRICA

PACIFIC OCEAN

OCEAN

INDIAN

OCEAN

AUSTRALIA

45

Find Out More

Books

Borgert-Spaniol, Megan. *Mongooses*. Minneapolis: Bellwether Media Inc., 2014.

Ciovacco, Justine. *Meerkats*. Pleasantville, NY: Reader's Digest Young Families, 2007.

Marsh, Laura F. *Meerkats*. Washington, DC: National Geographic Society, 2013.

Visit this Scholastic Web site for more information on meerkats:
www.factsfornow.scholastic.com
Enter the keyword **Meerkats**

Index

Page numbers in *italics* indicate a photograph or map.

About the Author

Josh Gregory is the author of more than 90 books for kids. He has written about everything from animals to technology to history. A graduate of the University of Missouri-Columbia, he currently lives in Portland, Oregon.